Talking to the Sky

Poems

Jamieson Wolf

This is a work of fiction. Names, characters, places, and incidents are products of the author's imagination or are used fictitiously and are not to be construed as real. Any resemblance to actual events, locales, organizations, or persons, living or dead, is entirely coincidental.

Talking to the Sky

Copyright© 2014 Jamieson Wolf

ISBN: 978-0-9917580-9-8

Cover Artist: Jamieson Wolf

Text: Jamieson Wolf

All rights reserved. No part of this book may be used or reproduced electronically or in print without written permission, except in the case of brief quotations embodied in reviews.

For Everyone.

PRAISE FOR JAMIESON WOLF

"Jamieson Wolf is a gifted writer!"
Kelley Armstrong, New York Times Best Selling Author

"As I read, Jamieson Wolf taught me to dance to the beats of his heart. Tender, heartbreaking and beautiful."
Caroline Smailes, Author of In Search of Adam, Black Boxes, Like Bees to Honey and The Drowning of Arthur Braxton

"Jamieson Wolf writes like Augusten Burroughs without the cynicism."
Nasim Marie Jafry, Author of The State of Me

PRAISE FOR TALKING TO THE SKY

"So expect the unexpected and be pleasantly surprised. Keep an open mind and heart and travel along with this author on a journey through life. Experience with him just what he has been living with and through this last year. I challenge you to change your thinking and attitude with this book. Bring on the adventure as you travel him and get Talking to the Sky yourself."
Elaine Breault

I have had the pleasure of reading this collection a few times and will many more I am sure. Jamieson's words provokes the entire spectrum of emotions in his words, allowing feelings to surface in the reader easily. There is an almost haunting permanence in the stories he weaves, one that has taken me to my own experiences that I thought were long lost. This poet is magical. His words are powerful and loving. A very very good read!!
Dava Gamble, Author of Silver Journey's and Silver Cusp

"With his unique style and powerful imagery, Jamieson Wolf lures us into this beautiful volume of poetry. Colors splash across the page, emotions are captured in a single word or phrase. We ride the city bus and see a woman's tears, feel the touch of a caring hand, experience the joy in a child's smile.

We walk a city street, hushed with snow. Friends and lovers meet with a warm breath on the cheek, a kiss, a sad goodbye. We witness courage, personal growth, moments of humor, strength, snatches of a dream.

Each poem is a stolen moment in time, raw, vivid, and intimate. Touching the Sky is an uplifting affirmation of life not soon forgotten."

Dianne Harstock, Author or Alex, Without Aiden and Philips Watcher

A Note About Talking to the Sky

There was a brief period in 2013 where I couldn't write. I was silent for a month.

The stories were still in my head though. The characters were still speaking. I was in and out of sleep in the beginning and when I wasn't awake to hear them, they filled my dreams.

As I started to get better, I would sit at the screen, willing my hands to work again. I used to be able to write 20,000 words in a weekend, thirty if I pushed it. Now I could barely write a few of them. All these voices were speaking at once, characters left unwritten.

I had lost my voice. Writing is how I speak to the world, how I put myself out there, how I engage with life. Day after day, as I stared at the keyboard and screen before me. It was like looking at a big fluffy cloud, and my mind was talking to it. It was the biggest writers block ever.

I did the only thing I could think of: turn to poetry. I willed my hands to work, one letter and one word at a time. Poems didn't have to be long, I could not write the same way, but I could still tell a story.

At times, I was able to type out a few lines, a couple of phrases. However, I was writing again.

That was enough.

These poems sprung out of the need to heal myself. As I continued to heal, the poems kept coming. Each poem through out the year was like a stepping stone on my path to finding me so that instead of talking to my computer, I was talking to the sky once more.

There are quite a few people in my life that helped me to get better through out 2013. This book is for them: WM and WD, Karine, Dava, Meaghan. Julie, Dawn, Erin, and Stephanie. Trevour, Heather, Jackie and my Tarot family. All I can say is thank you and hope that these words are enough in some small way to repay you for everything you've done for me

Jamieson

Difficulty Speaking

His words were heavy. They

tumbled

out of his mouth, hard consonants that

fall

like stones. His voice was dark with grief but it was his eyes that startled me.

Did I tell you that they killed him?

What happened?

I am frightened by him and my heart begins to

beat

faster. I could smell the stench of stale cologne and cigarettes on his skin. His eyes are brown rimmed with red. I wondered vaguely what he was on and how far he had

f

a

l

l

e

n

I wondered what he had given up.

I wondered if he would ever find inside of him what it took to out of his present circumstances.

Yep

He says.

Stupid shit went and bit a kid in the face.

He makes three motions, a hand like claws pawing his face. He makes three loud sounds and my heart

beats

faster. The noises he makes are comic book sound effects that are almost primal and terrifying coming out at such a slow speed:

Blam!

Pow!

Zamm!

I can hear the exclamation marks behind the words, teeth are in my flesh. Its teeth are

t

e

a

r

i

n

g

my skin. Then he

flicks

a lighter and the scene vanishes. There is a dark look in his eyes that tells me the pain has not healed yet.

My dog killed a fucking kid, man

He says.

I look into his eyes and see no hope left. He does not have a

d

r

o

p

left to spare

What Awaited Me

The bus was late.

And so I waited.

And waited some more.

A woman who looked

badly in need of a meal

smoked a cigarette

silently beside me.

An older woman

was talking to a gentleman

about the proper way

to grow tulips.

You have to stroke the bulbs before you plant them. Otherwise, they won't grow properly. You have to show them a little love, you know?

A man on a bike

Zoomed

by   me

His motion sounding

Like wind, or the

Whisper of something

tangible

The bus came and the

only free seat was near

a screaming woman.

She had a bandage on her

cheek that ran from below her

right eye and straight

down her face. Her eyes were glassy.

I am not sure if she was medicated.

She was raving, screaming as if

she was frightened of something,

she was distraught, yelling gibberish,

she was absolutely and completely

terrified.

Youdon'tknowwhattheydidtome,whattheytried todotome,butIfoughtthem,Ifought them,showedthemwhotheyweredealingwith

She made sounds that no human

should ever have to make. They

were horrible sounds. I don't think

I will ever forget the noise of them.

Her sounds defy description.

(sobbing)showed them who they were messingwith,thatIwouldn'ttaketheirshit.

Ifaughtthemdoyouunderstand?Ifaughtthosewhocouldnotbeslayed.I havetheirblooonmyskin

Instead of trying to help her,

I looked into my iPad. I was reading,

delving into a story. I was trying to.

But really, I wanted a window

to look into, so that I could

ignore the screaming that took place

across from me.

Every so often,

I'd look at the others,

my fellow passengers.

Some were staring openly,

some looked away.

But for the most part,

all I saw was a sea of windows,

cell phones and iPads and Kindles,

eReaders and Blackberries and more.

It was a sea of windows,

their screens lighting our faces,

their glow soft and comforting

highlighting

our

fear

of

her

One woman in front of her,

she reached out.

She put her hand on the frightened

woman's hand, laid it on fingers

that were gripping the iron bar

of the seat.

Her voice was surprisingly gentle.

It's going to be okay.

She said.

It's going to be okay.

__Bus Babies__

The girls are

fairly young, perhaps

sixteen or seventeen,

around that age.

They are carrying

baby carriers, it is

the third day in a row

that I've seen them.

They ride the bus

up front, always

talking, chit chatting,

about themselves.

Today, the woman

across from them

points

to the baby carriers,

her finger making

a sharp and deliberate

jab

into the air.

When I was in high school, we used an egg. Are they those life like ones that have the chip inside of them and make them cry?

The girls look at

the older woman.

They take her in.

I wonder what they

will say to her,

how they will

respond.

To my surprise,

and the shock of

everyone else on

the bus, the girls

respond to the

older woman with

polite, happy voices.

Yeah. We have to take parenting, its mandatory now.

In my day, that course was optional.

No, you have to take it now, as one of your electives, the other girl says.

You having an okay time with them? You're awfully young to be carrying babies, pretend or otherwise. They keep you up at night?

Yeah. The first girl again. *It's hard when you have to get up at night and rock them and shit.*

Her skin blushes

a bright pink

at the word,

her innocence

convincing,

her sincerity

sincere.

One is blond

and the other

is brunette. Other

than their hair,

they could be

sisters.

The other spoke,

the blond one,

her voice softer

this time, almost

contemplative.

Yeah, one of our friends accidentally killed her baby by dropping it a few times and once she dropped it in the bath tub and left it there. It fried the internal chip, so she just went and bought a new one and no one ever knew.

She takes a

moment to consider

this thought, her

eyes far away

and somewhat dreamy.

She's going to make such a great *mother.*

The older woman

looked at her

with a shocked

silence so loud

that I have

trouble

breathing.

Snippet Bees

He listened to people as he walked,

Their conversations flowing past him

In portions of conversation

That together made up a whole:

I was like....

...don't touch me there...

...you don't know where that's been...

...and so he was like...

...you can't just do that outright...

...no common sense at all...

...stupid bitch.

He tried to push past the words,

Tried to keep them at bay,

But they were like a cloud

That hung over my head.

I thought briefly of

A bear with a balloon,

Dressed like a cloud.

But this cloud

Did not want honey.

Instead the bees wanted to

Tear

Past his skin,

So they could get

To the sweet nectar of

His words that rested

Somewhere under the surface:

> *I can't believe...*
>
> *...how fucking stupid he was...*
>
> *...what did he think would happen...*
>
> *...aggravating the powers that be...*
>
> *...such a good boy...*
>
> *...such a good little boy...*
>
> *...little shit...*

He tries again

To keep them out,

Words that are not his,

That do not belong to him.

But the bees have come,

They have

                                        Ripped

Through his skin,

Until he is overflowing

With words that

Are not his own.

A Casual Vacancy

She looked at the book, with its bright coloured cover, as if she were allowed to read again. I think I recognized somewhere that she was kin, that she was a

kindred spirit

In truth, I thought she was coming on to me for a second. She had that glazed look about her, as if she were ultimately happy. I wondered when I had last seen that look.

I know it's going to be amazing.

She said.

Because it's her, it's J. K. Rowling. No, it won't be Harry Potter, but then again, what else will ever be?

She was holding the same book I held in my hand.

I haven't even read the reviews, except those stupid one star reviews for the price of the eBook. It's not good to rate a book that way; it brings the value of the work down.

She smiled and touched my arm. My shoulder, squeezed it slightly.

No,

She said.

Don't read the reviews. Just enjoy it for what it is.

She looked me deep in the eye.

Just enjoy it.

She said again.

 I wondered if, like me, it was the first physical book in months. Everything else had been on a screen. He wondered if she would go home and devour it, or wait for the right moment to actually open a book and

dip

into its pages.

I will.

I said.

I'll make sure to do that.

Then I went home and read the eBook.

Smoke

The first customer took his cigarettes

from the cashier and I could already

see him

puffing

away on a fresh cigarette. The next

customer went up and the cashier

asked him for ID

I don't have any fucking

Identification.

He said.

You have to show ID,

The cashier said.

I always buy here, the new

customer said. *You ask*

your fucking manager,

you ask him and he'll

tell you to sell to me,

he'll fucking tell you.

He said.

No ID, no smokes.

The cashier said.

This is fucking

discrimination,

that's what this is.

You won't sell to me

cus you don't like me,

cus I'm a transsexual.

That has nothing to do

with any of it.

Then why didn't you card

that other fucking guy?

He asked.

Why didn't you card him?

He looked older than you.

The cashier replied.

Fucking discrimination.

He said.

I sided up to the counter

and asked for my own

brand of cigarettes.

There was no request

for identification. No

demand for me to prove

who I was.

I walked out the store,

with the nasal voice

of the transsexual

fluttering in my wake.

Why didn't you

fucking card him either?

Fucking racist!

As I left the store

I wondered whether

the customer was right:

Was the cashier

withholding cigarettes

because the customer

was a transsexual?

Or was the customer

blowing smoke

up his own ass?

Happy Colour

The shop was in ruins.

Sheets covered the stone steps

like flattened ghosts,

soft, yet promising something

that was darker.

I tried to get what I needed,

but there were shelves and

racks in my way. They

blocked my path

like silent giants.

I moved and stepped around them,

I wondered if I looked

as if I were dancing with

something only I could see.

At the counter, the clerk

took my card, I got what I needed.

The painters around us

were going about their work

as if we weren't there.

A customer in line behind me

smiled as I made my purchase.

It's going to be a happy colour.

He said.

The walls around us

were being painted

a solid yellow. The colour of

gold leaf that gets

caught by that perfect

beam of autumn sunshine.

I nodded.

Smiled back.

Yes,

it is.

I replied.

Yellow Bottle

You're going to ride the fastest machines known to man.

His voice came out

like a fog horn

startling the

early dark morning.

His jacket was

bright yellow,

like sun caught

on his skin.

They've been made faster than before, stronger than before, better than before. We can rebuild him, we can make him better.

There was a

bottle in his hand,

clutched as if

it were a life line

to something

we couldn't see.

The small crowd of us

waiting for the bus

to arrive avoided

looking at him.

We didn't want to

encourage him,

acknowledge him.

We looked

away, down, through

him but we

could still hear

his voice as

it echoed

in the darkness.

They can rebuild me. They can fix what's wrong with me, ladies and gentleman. They can fix me, rebuild me, make me stronger than before. I'll gain back everything I've lost, everything that was taken from me. You're going to ride the fastest machines known to man.

When he

looked at us

to see if he

had a captive

audience.

We averted

our eyes.

Red Paint

I heard the

screaming first, like

someone was

      ripping

sound out of the

his throat. It

was difficult to

understand him

at first, hard to

make out the

words he

      spewed

forth like blood.

I half expected it

to dot the pavement

like red paint.

> *....You think you're fucking better than me? You think that? Well fucking think again asshole. I fucking told you not to say anything and what do you do? You go and open your fucking mouth. I TOLD you not to say anything, I fucking told you.*

The answering reply

is a soft mumble.

It takes me a moment

to realize that the

man is talking to

what I first thought

was a piece of shadow.

The shadow moves,

tries to go towards

the angry one,

mumbling something

unintelligible:

> *I just….mumble mumble….didn't mean to…never told me that…didn't mean to…not just me, not at all, in fact….mumble…not at all, I didn't….not at all.*

He reminded me

of the Raven,

caught and hidden

inside shadow,

gossamer threads

of darkness

pulled together

into shape.

The non shadow man

lunged, his face

momentarily highlighted

by a splash of light

even as a slice

of moonlight

could be seen

in his hand.

The blade,

the slice

of moonlight

sliced

into the mumbling man,

blood like the paint

that had filled my

imagination

spilling

forth from

his skin

I told you

He said.

I mother fucking told *you.*

Past Resident

They stood in my doorway,

momentary shadows that

stood like sentries to

the world beyond.

"You know about the guy who used to live here, right?"

This was the one on the right.

"No, you mean the guy before me?" I asked. "The previous resident?"

"No, the one before him."

"The past resident."

This was the other.

His voice was deep,

as if it came from

the deep down,

from the shadows

that laid within.

"There was something wrong with him."

"Real shame, though,

what happened to him."

"What?" I tried to keep

the note of panic

out of my voice.

I try, but I am not

entirely successful.

"Why? What happened

to him?"

"Killed himself."

He took a breath

between his words.

"He wasn't right in the head."

He is Everywhere

I got off the bus

and she was there,

a scarf wrapped

around her face,

its red colour faded.

She looks familiar,

like someone I

had seen before.

"Brother Jamon?" She says to me. *"Are you just coming from work?"*

I can hardly hear her

over the noise and

racket of the busses,

I have to lean in close.

"I'm sorry?"

She looks at me,

taken aback,

as if seeing me

for the first time.

"I'm sorry." She says. "You look so much like my dear Brother Jamon."

She holds out

her hands and

takes in all of me

from head to toe

in one gesture.

"From your clothes to the way you look. I am sorry! I thought you were him. He is my Brother with God. He had a hard life, had a terrible time, but he let the Lord find him."

I should have been

shocked at her words,

should have been

walking away.

But she had put a

hand on my arm.

Her eyes were warm,

her voice was soothing.

"I'm sorry." I said. "I'm Jason. My name is Jason."

"It's okay." She replied. "It doesn't matter what your name is. If God found my Brother Jamon, he knows where you are, too. Even if you don't know him well enough to invite him over for dinner."

"It doesn't matter. God is everywhere."

She smiled brightly

at me, that smile

filling me up,

not with

religious fever

but with joy.

"Yes, he is. Yes, but you have to let him in so that he can help you. If Jamon did, so can you."

Her hand

on my arm

gave a little

squeeze, a pulse

of comfort.

"These times will end, but until then, you have to remain strong."

"It's okay." I said. "All I can do is take it one day at a time."

These words

rewarded me with

another

of her smiles.

"Yes," She said. *"One day at a time."*

Translation

She looked up when the

other woman entered,

filling the bar with a

wretched scent. She

put a smile on her

face.

Darling. You look lovely*Shit, bitch, you got fucking fat.*

It had been twelve years

Since she had seen her.

Sweetheart, you're looking well. How's Walter?/*Who's he fucking now instead of you?*

They sat down and smiled

at each other. An awkward

silence ensued, just a

                        moment

Then they smiled, laughed

And she wondered if they

had made a mistake,

meeting like this.

There was so much she

wanted to say. So much

she would not.

You look so good! When did you get so thin!/*Probably puked it all up before you came over, you fucking bitch.*

Oh, I did the medically supervised diet. Where you just have shakes.\/*I look better than you, you fat ugly slut.*

You haven't aged a day since high school/*Yeah, you look like a dried out she hag then, too.*

Sweetheart, you're too kind\and you're full of shit.

They take a sip of

their drinks, letting the

bubbles float on their

tongues. The words

sizzle on their skin.

This time, the

moment is longer

stretching for more

than a single beat

of silence.

They try again,

smiling. She wonders

where the waiter

is with their

drinks or if

they will have

to fend for

themselves.

So what are you doing with yourself now?/*I take it you're still on welfare?*

Oh, writing a novel.*Which is more than you'll ever do, you dried up old husk.*

How interesting!/*Don't make me laugh!*

Yes, it's quite fun. I've already got an agent/*Ha! Take that Bitchzilla!*

What's it about?/*Like I give a flying fuck.*

It's a romance novel. They're all the rage right now./*It's about what you did to me, truth disguised as fiction.*

How lovely./*Ugh, probably some fucking Fifty Shades of Grey mommy porn.*

The silence stretches

for a very

lengthy time, the

moment too long

to be covered

by laughter and

smiles that do

not reach their

eyes. She wonders

at all they

have said and

all that is

left unspoken.

Translucent Wish

He watched him.

A cigarette was

dangling from his

fingertips. He took

a swig of his beer.

The thing is,

you have to

imagine what it

was like, always

wondering if they

would find you,

if they would

see. You know?

I didn't know.

His words painted

translucent pictures in

my imagination. They

filled my head

with dreams of

darkness and blackness.

We had to be

so very quiet.

People were on

the street, dressed

in black. There

was a brigade

of women that

ran along the

rooftops, with buckets.

They were filled

with water. One

flame, boy, one

flame would be

enough to set

us ablaze completely.

Yet there he

sat with flame

in hand. I

marvelled at his

braveness. I hoped

to one day

be so brazen.

There was this

one woman. Man,

she was awful

with the water.

Kept spilling it

all over herself.

Couldn't put out

a fire if

her life depended

upon it!

He took another

puff off of

his cigarette. It

glowed red like

the sun, bright

like a wish

yet to bloom

into being, there
one moment and
gone the next.
She was shit
with water, but
man could she
ever shoot a
gun! Took down
three planes, each
with a single
bullet. Got the
propeller every time!
He let out
smoke this time
and I wondered
if the flame
was somehow giving
him strength. If
it filled him
up with a

light that burned

bright in him.

Man, could she

ever fucking shoot.

Mirrored Pieces of the Same Thought

We sat around

a three legged

table. I could

smell the beer

on him. I

sat gingerly on

the seat. Careful.

                                       I don't get it at all man.

                No, listen.

The third man

leaned forward and

the table tipped.

          Goddamned mother fucking three legged table.

                                      Hey. Don't dis my table.

But you don't get it. What we remember now is not what we remembered then. What we thought we would know years down the road, we've forgotten. Just like we'll forge this conservation that we're having right now. It, too, will slip away from us.

I was entrance

by him. I

didn't know his

name. I took

in his scruffy

appearance, his dishevelled

hair and face.

<u>What do you mean? Of course we'll remember.</u>

We will, but only sort of. We'll become mirrored

fragments of thoughts. They will blend into one

another. We'll never be sure if we went to the

prom with Cindy or Claire. We'll forget

what our grandmother uses to smell

like. Everything will reflect off

each other.

There was silence

after this statement,

where all that

could be heard

were the clouds

of smoke being

released over our

heads, like blue

coloured thoughts.

                                                The hell you say?

But I thought

I understood him,

at least partially.

<u>We try to remember everything, to hold on to it, but time warps it.</u>

<u>As hard as we try to remember something, it slips away from us.</u>

<u>However we attempt to remember, each memory becomes a reflection.</u>

<u>They become a mirror to the one before it, mirrored pieces</u>

<u>that are all the same.</u>

                          The fuck man. You're both fucking crazy.

                                                          Yes

He said to

me, light of

a kindred spirit

in his eyes.

On the Yellow Brick Road

It's as if we

Found each other

On the Yellow Bick Road.

I was making my way

through the dark forest

(*The Scarecrow*

had run off,

leaving behind only

the sound of

rustling leaves

and wet straw.

He needed courage

instead of brains. Fucker).

The flapping crack

of the Winged Monkey's

could be heard above.

Clutching my basket

(*What did I have*

in there *anyway?*

I mean, who carries

a basket *anymore?)*

I made my way

deeper into the trees,

the bricks leaving

yellow scuff marks

on my shoes.

I wondered how

one washed ruby slippers,

(They were more

like leather boots,

sleek and wonderful.

They were made

from red leather

and had a line of

rubies along the toe.

Are rubies like rhinestones?)

or if they were

best left alone.

A sound to my left

drew my attention,

the small dog

in my arms

growling softly

(Fuck, I thought.

Fucking shit.

Please don't let

that be a Winged Monkey,

please, please, please!)

as a shadow detached

itself from the darkness

and came towards me.

The Wicked Witch

stood in front of me,

her green skin

blending in with

the leaves around her.

"Poppies," She said.

"Poppies will make

you sleep."

Her voice made

me want to

puncture my

ear drums.

Instead of her

voice, I wanted

instead the absence

of sound.

"You and your

fucking poppies."

Another voice said.

And then I saw you.

You didn't step

out of the darkness

so much as simply

outshine it.

light streamed

through the air,

its brilliance filling

the dark forest

until no shadows

remained to be seen.

It took me a moment

to realize that

the light came

only from you.

At first I thought

That you were

the Tin Woodsman.

But then I saw him,

trying to coax

a yellow brick

that had come loose

from the road

into conversation.

(*That Tin Man needed*

brains instead of

a heart. I wondered

how I had become

the travelling companion

of two men who

should not exist,

but were stupid

anyways).

I turned around

and there you were,

blond hair shining

bright in the dark.

In one hand

you held the

 Tin Woodman's axe.

It sliced through the air,

a whistle that

shimmered through the

air with sparks.

The arch ended

with a muffled thump.

I looked down and

the Wicked Witch

was looking up at me.

When you took my hand

to help me up,

magic beyond

all of Oz

flowed through us,

as though the

air was alive.

There was another

rustle from the trees

(*How many damned*

things are in

these woods, for

goodness sake?

Fuck, I thought.

I mean, really?)

and you pushed me

behind you, your

bloody axe already

at the ready.

The shape of

a large beast,

part lion, part man,

came through the

trees, growling.

(*That's it.* I thought.

The next vacation

I take will be

somewhere without

animals or a

woman with a

very serious epidermal

problem who wanted

to kill me and

take my fucking

ruby slippers.)

"Get behind me," You said.

"I'll protect you."

I didn't need to

for with you

by my side,

I was already

home sweet

home.

The Names We Choose to Call Ourselves

I tried to

concentrate on my

novel, tried to

read the words

swimming in front

of my eyes

but the conversation

of the people

sitting beside me

would keep intruding

So I was like, bitch, don't make me take out my cock and beat you with it.

What?

(Huff) *I'm talking about your big cock.*

I try to

Ignore them, try

to hide inside

the words of

my book but

their voices are

loud. There are

six of them

sitting in multiple

seats, talking across

the air to

each other. I

wonder if their

words have any

sort of colour.

Whatever. You shouldn't talk like that on a bus. What if someone hears you?

Fuck you very much.

It's true. One time I was riding with Poppit and he was talking about all of his bitches he was dating and turns out all of them, TwoTone, FishTaco, Ladygirl, Pleeb,

Rainbow and Brita were all on the bus behind him.

And what happened? TrebbleCleff was there too right? What did she say?

Well that's just it. Turns out Trebble was preggers with Poppit's baby.

No way.

Way.

So what happened?

Well Trebble didn't say anything, but she sent Coffee and Cake over to kick the shit out of Poppit.

Totally?

Totally. She sent Raygun and Peaches to help.

I wondered if

they were all

super heroes, if

they all had

secret identities that

they had forgotten

to change into.

Or maybe I

was a super

hero, here to

save the day.

You got any spare smokes, ChickenHawk?

Yeah.

Can I have one?

What's the magic word TastyBurger?

Fuck you very much.

I came to realize

There was no

way that these

kids were really

named ChickenHawk

or TastyBurger.

They were the

names they had

chosen out of

the air, the

names they chose

to call themselves,

rather than the

ones they were

given. I wondered

when their chosen

moniker will start

to lose its

lustre and allure.

Why were you talking about my big cock?

Magic Stick

Someone saw me

opening it on

the bus. I

had waited all

day. It lay

in my bag

like a beacon

of glee waiting

to be free.

What that?

What?

That.

It's an Ollivander's Box

What?

I took it

out, slid the

box open carefully,

lifted out the

prize within its

red velvet interior.

What is that? A stick?

It's a Harry Potter wand.

So it's a magic stick.

You totally don't care do you?

Not really.

You know it

won't actually do

any magic,

don't you?

Yes, I know it's just a pretend wand.

But later, I

wondered if it

could be. I

mean this was

Harry's wand, right?

Alone in my

apartment, I took

the wand carefully

out of the

Ollivander's box, slipped

it out of

the red velvet

interior. I knew

that normally the

wand chose the

wizard, that if

it were real,

there would be

a glow or

a fuzzy hum

moving through my

skin when I

picked it up.

There was none.

I hadn't expected

any, not really.

But when I

waved the wand

through the air

speaking the words

EXPECO PATRONUM!

and a bright

light filled my

apartment, I knew

then that magic

was real indeed.

Cock of the Walk

The sky is

dark at this

hour, the sun

yet to rise.

I am about

to light a

cigarette before I

see him. He

taps me on

the shoulder softly.

"Can I have one of those?"

I recognize him.

He is a

neighbour, someone from

the building next

door. I don't

know his name

and we have

only spoken vague

hellos before. He

leans in closer

and I hand

him a cigarette.

I can smell

the booze off

of him, can

see it in

him as he

begins to sway

even as he

stands still. He

looks at me.

"You still with your man?"

"Yes."

"How long has that been now?"

"Almost two years."

"Huh."

He regards me

for a moment

with bleary eyes.

"I liked to get my cock sucked."

"What?"

"I like it when guys ride it too. You know where I live, right?"

"Unfortunately."

"I'm totally in to being fucked. You come by if you want to hop on my dick."

I have no

words to this.

It is as

if he has

taken them from

me, one word

for each step

he takes, stumbling,

away into darkness.

Memory Speech

What I miss

most about not

being able to

talk is the

conversations I would have.

I would be

able to float

in and out

of dialogues that

would fill me

with plenty of

words till I

was so full

of them they

flowed from me.

How was your day?
Fine, how was yours?
I had the oddest thing happen to me.

I remember words

instead, fill my

memory with words.

Oh really? Do tell

Well it was the strangest thing. I got off the bus and a lady gave me a flower

Did you know this woman?

I am full
with words that
can't find a
valid release. So
instead, I take
mental photographs of
the sound patterns.
So that I don't forget.

Never seen her before in my life. She was a complete stranger to me.
Well, what did she do? Did she attack you or something?
No, nothing like that. She gave me a rose.
A flower?
Do you know any other kind? Yes, a flower.
So that's it? Some crazy lady hands you flower?
I think it's nice. A random act of kindness.
Please you don't know where that flowers been. Did you Lysol it first?
Oh you.

I hate Zombies....

He said. His

voice was thick

with something that

was either booze

or drugs, perhaps

a mixture of

both. He wobbled

a little, as

if a strong

breeze would knock

him over. For

a moment, it

didn't look like

he was going

to answer. His

face was a blank

slate. I wondered

if he was

really the zombie.

I don't like them. They're so far from our reality.

Well, of course they are, that's part of the appeal.

You mean to tell me you ran all the way out here for people dressed like zombies?

Yeah, he said there was like a parade or something. I brought my camera.

Man,

he said giving

me a look

that said I

was an idiot.

I've never seen anyone run to the zombies. They usually run away from them.

Saying nothing, I

went back into

my building letting

the door close

with a click.

I made my

way back to

my apartment and

decided to watch

some of The

Walking Dead.

Mobile Books

We waited for

the bus, hoping

that it would

come. It had

been thirty minutes

and three buses

were supposed to

have come. It

was a very long

half hour. We

stood there, all

of us, looking

at our watches.

"I wonder when the bus will come. The man on the phone said it would be another fifteen minutes."

She huffed out

a breath of

impatience. She held

her cell phone

in one clutched

fist. She looked

royally pissed off.

"I mean, he didn't even tell me what had caused the delay. He said that one of the buses had been removed. I mean what does that mean?"

Something rang in

her purse. She

stared at the

phone in her

hand and then

at her bag.

She looked up

at me, disbelief

on her face.

"What's that? Why isn't my phone ringing?"

"You better look and see."

I said. The

woman reached into

her bag with

slightly shaking fingers.

She was quick

though and had

her hand in

and out of

her bag in

a flash. In

her hands, she

held a small

paperback book. She

gazed at the

ringing book with

an "o" of

wonder shaping her

lips. The cover

of the book

had a title

emblazoned on its

front in gold.

She stroked the

cover as if

it were a

treasured pet or

friend; something

she was offering

comfort to, or

perhaps receiving it.

"The Princess Bride."

There was a

longing in her

voice, it looked

like she was

about to cry.

"*I haven't read this in years. It was my very favourite book in my younger days.*"

She opened the

cover and the

ringing stopped immediately.

A voice spoke

out from the

books pages. It

was strong and

full of longing.

"As you wish…"

The woman started

to read right

away. She looked

up when other

bags and pockets

started to ring.

Soon the air

was full ringing

and several voices

speaking at once.

Buzz!

"We'll be Friends Forever, won't we, Pooh?'

Ping!

"I'm so glad I live in a world where there are Octobers."

Ring!

"Some people without brains do an awful lot of talking, don't you think?"

Sing!

"Love is a great beautifier."

Zing!

"It is good people who make good places"

The woman looked

at me, fear

replacing the wonder

that was there

a moment ago.

"What's going on? Why are the books ringing like mobile phones? Who's talking to us? What do you think this means?"

There was a

note of panic

in her voice

now whereas before,

there had been

only fatigue. I

thought of how

to answer her,

how I should

respond to her

question. I shrugged

and smiled softly.

"I think it means the bus will be a while."

I said, just

as my own

pocket started ringing.

Heart Shaped Box

When I lost

my heart, I

went looking for

it. I didn't

find it in

any of the

usual places: behind

the sofa, by

the bed, on

the dresser, in

my pants pockets.

I had no idea

where it was

and was beginning

to get worried;

it hadn't strayed

so far from

home before. There

was a knock

at my door.

When I answered

the summons, I

opened the door

to find you

standing there. I

blinked and felt

hot and flushed.

"Yes?"

I said. You

looked at me

with a smile

in your eyes.

"I think I have something that belongs to you."

You said, reaching

Into your coat.

You pulled out

a small box

shaped like a

valentine. Inside, my

heart lay nestled

amid a bed

of satin. I

reached out and

touched my heart.

It pulsed as

If it sensed

me close by.

"How did you find it? How did you find me?"

I tried to

keep the need

out of my

voice, the hum

that moved through

my entire body,

the thrum that

pulsed where my

heart should be.

"I found it beside me when I woke. I picked it up and held it, put it in the heart shaped box. It's like a compass. It grew brighter when I was facing the right direction."

I stared at

you, into your

grey blue eyes.

I saw an

ocean there, deep

and calming, wanting

to slip into

it and let

the water caress

my tired skin.

"What did it lead you to?"

"You."

I held out

my hand and

picked up my

heart. It lay

there in my

palm for a

moment before disappearing.

Inside my chest,

I felt something

beat once more.

When I looked

at you again,

my heart beat

quickly, filling my

skin with shivers.

"How can my heart lead you to me?"

You regarded me

for a moment

and smiled before

you moved closer.

"The heart works in mysterious ways, doesn't it?"

When you kissed

me, all thoughts

of compass hearts

and valentine shaped

boxes fled my

mind. My heart

beat again in my

chest, strong and

true. I knew

that with you

beside me, my

heart would never

wander far again.

When Love Blooms

We are in

a glade with

stars that glow

like diamonds in

the sky. There

are trees that

surround us, their

leaves moving in

a breeze, whispering

sweet nothings to

us. He stands

beside me and

holds something out

for me to

look at. He

hands it to

me. It's a

branch covered in

closed up flowers.

It's as if

they are sleeping.

"Look what we can do together."

He says to

me. He puts

hand over mine

and we're holding

the branch together.

Nothing happens for

a moment, a

heartbeat of time.

Then the trees

begin to rustle

and the branch

we're holding starts

to glow. Blue

magic moves up

the branch and

all the flowers

begin to open.

They are alight

with a bright

white glow that

throws our faces

into sharp relief.

The light brightens,

all the flowers

begin to open

until they are

full and bright

and filled with

magic. I look

at him and

down at our

hands clasped around

the flowers stem.

"How is a thing like this possible?"

He looks at

me with a

smile that warms

my cold heart.

"Anything is possible, when love blooms."

A Parade for Two

I locked my

apartment door. My

neighbour came out

of his apartment.

There's a parade and a band outside man!

Yeah, right. What for?

I don't know, but I heard it through my window.

I had not

heard anything. My

windows were closed

against the heat

and to keep

the A/C in.

Who cares man! It's a parade! There giving out beads and food and everything!

I followed him

upstairs and outside.

There, moving in

of us, there

was a mass

of people. My

neighbour and I

move down to

the sidewalk. We

stare at the

sea of people.

What are they parading for?

I don't know man, Some of them have signs, look!

I look and

indeed they do,

but they look

like bed sheets

held up on

sticks. They

are smeared with

blood. I look

at my neighbour's

face and see

the same look

of abject horror.

What the fuck man?

He says quietly.

I mean, seriously?

I don't know

what to say,

so I just

shake my head.

It is then

that I notice

the people. They

are all in

some sort of

decay, limbs torn,

blood thick and

thick in the

air. I turn

to my neighbour

and motion at

the people that

are walking by .

What the hell is going on? And why aren't any of them attacking us?

I turn to him,

looking away from

the crowd. Again

I don't know

what to say,

so I say

exactly that instead.

I don't know.

When we turn

around, a crowd

of them surrounds

us, looking at

both of us

with white eyes.

Gambling Train

The train moves

along the tracks,

moving at speeds

that force the

surrounding countryside to

blur. The drink cart

has been by

and I can

hear the sounds

of people and

children crying. I

am sitting next

to my boyfriend,

enjoying the quiet.

A voice breaks

out on my

left. It is

an older woman.

"Almost twenty stops on this tour of Canada, and not one of them are at a casino."

I turn around

and look to

my right. It's

a sea of

white hair and

wrinkles The woman

speaks once more.

"The booze cart is already gone. I wonder if I asked them whether or not they'd leave the bottle.

I laugh despite

myself and the

woman turns to

look at me.

I give her

a sheepish grin

and a shrug.

"Sorry, I was just thinking the same thing."

"Will they?"

"What?"

"Leave the bottle?"

"No, probably not."

"Bastards."

She says this

with a smile.

"Where you all from?"

"Where we're going to. I was born there".

"You from Ottawa?"

"Yes."

"Is there a casino?"

"Not till next year, but there's tons of fun stuff to do."

"Where are you staying? "

My boyfriend says.

"The Chateau Laurier."

"Fancy. I live here and I've never stayed there."

Just tell a cab to take you to Casino Lac Lemy.

"They have slots?"

Yes, 5 cent, 10 cent, 25 cent. I think they even have penny slots.

"Now that's a tourist attraction!"

"But there's also the light show at Parliament Hill, the Rideau Canal Locks, tons of bus tours and museums…"

"Honey, we're old and we have money to burn. We like to gamble, even if we don't win."

"I've never seen the point."

"Honey, the possibility is the point. Anything is possible if you believe hard enough."

I can think

of nothing to

say to that.

So I listen

to the rumbling

of the train

as it carries

us back home.

Non/Smoker

How is the non-smoking going?

Good. It's been since June.

I really hate smokers. They infect the environment.

It's early in

the morning and

I haven't had

coffee yet. I

don't want to

have a philosophical

conversation before I

have coffee. I

just nod, hoping

he'll shut up.

I mean, smokers don't understand. They're infecting everyone's health. I just want to punch them.

You can't think like that. Everyone has a vice.

Yes, but these people pay for their vice and make other people suffer.

People buy booze, drugs and porn too. They're not hurting anyone.

But smokers are. Have you ever had an inflamed lung?

No.

That's because you were a smoker. Your body has built an immunity to the smoke. It's different for people who don't smoke at all.

I really wish

he'd shut up.

There are two

people near us

at the bus

stop that I

work with. Both

of them are

smokers. I try

to think of

something to say.

But anything I

do say will

keep him going.

I needn't have

worried. He's on

a roll and

keeps on preaching.

I mean, don't they realize that they're the reason for global warming? Every time I see a smoker at work, or eating at a picnic table, I tell them to move on, that no one wants to eat their smoke.

I don't know

what to say

to this, but

he looks at

me and I realize

he expects me

to say something.

Patios are the worst. All of them smoking just outside of the patio, I mean, don't they realize that the smoke finds the non smokers anyway through the air?

I am actually

embarrassed for him.

I finally find

my voice. I

don't know what

I will say

until the words

fly out of

my open mouth

You can't blame smokers for the world's problems. Everyone smokes for a reason at first but then they become addicted. They can't help it and it's so hard to quit.

They should make is illegal and arrest anyone who smokes. They're killing the world.

Maybe you should smoke.

I can't do that! I might get throat cancer and lose my voice!

That would be an improvement.

I walk forward

to my bus

that has arrived.

Enjoy your day.

I tell him,

and he looks

at me blankly.

1Q84/His

We are in

a parking lot.

There is a

man watching us

from a short

distance away, standing

behind a small

booth. It has

golden awning covered

in stripes. There

is a sign

below the counter

that says: **MAGIC!**

DELIGHT! WONDERS! CHEAP!

I turn to

my him with

a quizzical look.

"What do you think he's selling?"

"I don't know. But I don't like the look of him. He unsettles me."

I can instantly

see what he

means. The man

has sallow looking

skin, pointy shining

teeth and eyes

that see too

much. He sees

us looking and

beckons to us.

"Come on boys! The sales are rolling today! What do you want? Wealth? Riches? Come one come all!"

"We're the only ones here."

"Then you'll be the only ones to benefit! Come on boys! Come up and let me see you!"

We walk towards

the sallow skinned

man. He smiles

at us with

a mouth that

looks big enough

to eat us.

"I can see you're both literary types! Yes I can, you both have brains the size of basket balls. Don't play dumb with me for I always know! You-"

He points to

my him with

a long finger.

"You'd be a teacher at some fancy pants school, wouldn't you?"

"How did you know that?"

"I told you, I always know. And you-"

He points to

me and it

seems like his

fingernails are growing.

"You'd be a fancy pants author, telling and spinning yarns and telling tales."

"There's no way you could know that."

"I always know, I always do. Just as I know that you're very much in love and your love grew out of reading the same book. You met at a book group where a bunch of fancy pants people like yourselves were reading the same thing."

I'm starting to

grow afraid now.

I look at

my him and

he has the

same look of

panic that I

do. Fear runs

though my body.

"I can give you the symbol your love grew out of if you want it. **THE MOON!**"

He yells these

words like a

circus performer and

I cringe. But

then he raises

his arms to

the sky and

lowers them with

a grand flourish.

"There gentleman, there! It's the symbol of your love that grew from nothing. It's going for cheap. It's slightly used, you understand, hundreds of thousands of years old, but I'll let you have it at a great price!"

I look up

and there, sliding

down from the

sky is the

moon, green with

hints of gold.

I take his

hand inside of

my own, feeling

awe instead of

fear, reverence instead

of dread. I

feel only wonder.

The symbol of

our love hanging

above us, waiting

to be discovered.

I turn to

the man who

always knows and

point at the

moon with my

one free hand.

"How much?"

Dreaming Awake

"It was such a nice dream. It was filled with satin and all things soft."

The older woman

sat at the

front of the

bus, holding onto

a striped parasol

even though it

wasn't raining.

"My Nan was in the dream. She told me to comb my hair, that it looked like a birds nest. In the dream, a family of birds had taken refuge there."

I looked around

to see who

she was talking

to. An old

man sat next

to her but

had his head

turned away. She

could only be

talking to herself.

"I was protecting the birds, so they sat on my head like a living crown. I had a beautiful gown, covered in pearls and other fabrics."

She reached up

to pat her

hair and I

reflected that it

did look like

a birds nest.

She was also

wearing a polka-dot

skirt, high heeled

boots and a

robins egg blue

sweater. Some people

looked as if

they wanted to

quiet her, but

I hoped they

didn't. She looked

so happy talking

of the dream

within herself. I

didn't want her

to lose the

smile that was

so incredibly bright.

"The dress was made of satin and of other things. I danced while the birds sang for me. I carried my own orchestra with me! Such a beautiful dream."

She got off

the bus and

I watched her

walk away, dancing

slightly, listening to

the dream music

that was still

inside her head.

Mirror Me

I do not

own a full

length mirror. I

have one small

mirror where only

my face is

visible. Every time

I look in

a full length

mirror, I see

myself as I

used to be,

close to three-hundred

pounds and very

unhappy. And every

time I look

into the glass,

my mirror me

is there inside

my head, speaking.

You are nothing. You are a fat slob. You're worth nothing, you're a piece of shit.

Mirror Me takes

over the mirror

and his body

and face cover

my own until

I don't exist.

You're pathetic, don't you know that everyone laughs at you? No one loves you.

Even after all

I have accomplished,

all I have

done, I can

still hear his

voice, still see

his sneering face.

I try to

turn a deaf

ear, frustrated that

after all the

pounds I've shed,

all the doubts

I've vanished, that

he's still there.

You're silly to think anyone could love you. You're stupid, you're ugly, you're nothing.

So when I

do look in

a full length

mirror, or any

pane of glass,

and start to

hear his voice,

I picture the

glass shattering, cracking

into a million

pieces, filling the

air with diamonds.

I yell at

the Mirror Me,

scream at him

inside my head.

I'M BEAUTIFUL! I'M LOVED! I AM FABULOUS! I AM AWESOME! I AM NOT DEFINED BY MY SCARS!

And Mirror Me,

his face fading

away into the

ether, has gone

silent until the

next time he

comes calling. I

repeat the words

to myself like

a holy mantra.

I am beautiful, I am loved, I am awesome, I am fabulous. I am beautiful, I am loved, I am awesome, I am fabulous. I am beautiful, I am loved, I am awesome, I am fabulous.

Next time he

comes to the

glass, I'll be

ready for him.

G and the D in an E

When the elevator

doors opened, G

was already there.

We have to stop meeting like this. He said.
The D snorted.

I suppose you want to go up.
G inclined his head.

Yes, and I suppose you want to go down.
The D snorted again.

Where else is there for me to go? You sent me to this cesspool remember?
G's voice was kind but stern.

Yes, I did, as you constantly remind me.
The D snorted

For a third time.

I hate it here. You know I can only get basic cable.
G inclined his head once more.

You know that the higher cable packages are only for the enlightened. Of which you are not.
The D grimaced.

You constantly remind me of that, too.
G smiled.

Yes. I do.
The D scowled.

Let's go down.
Up.
Down.
Up.
Fine.
There was steel in the D's voice.

Let's let the next wayward soul who boards decide our direction.
G nodded.

Fine. I am amenable to that.

The elevator stopped

and the doors

pinged and slid

open, revealing

a very sorry

looking man. He

had blood on

his clothes and

it was caked

into his fingernails.

Looks like we're going down then?
The D's words were full of smile.

G only smiled.

He let the

man covered in

blood onto the

elevator. Reaching out,

G took the

man's hands in

his and looked

into his eye.

Do you repent? G said. Do you seek forgiveness for what you've done?

Tears leaked out

of the mans

eyes and they

were filled with

a beautiful light.

<u>Yes.</u> The man said. <u>Yes.</u>

The D snorted

as the elevator

began to move

upwards, filling with

light as it

went. The D

snorted a final

time, grimacing at G.

You use the same trick every time.
G smiled.

And yet, you fall for it every time, do you not?
The D growled

as the light

in the elevator

began to burn

and singe his

skin.

Bastard. The D said.

Word Picture

Outside, it is
full of silence.
The quiet is
something that you
can almost touch,
almost a sound
in itself. A
book is open
on my lap.
The sun is
bright but I
am in the
shade, listening to
street noises and
the wind ruffling
the leaves. It
begins to sound
like it's own
kind of music.
For a moment,
it's nice just
to sit and
close my eyes
and revel in

this silence broken
only by the
sounds of others
moving and living
around me. Then
the silence is
broken by the
sound of pages
rustling. I look
down and the
book in my
lap sounds like
the leaves in
the trees. When
the pages stop
moving, I expect
to see words.
Instead, I see
a cobbled London
street. I can
see a bar
and there are
dark people entering
it. A man
off to the

side of the
word picture beckons
to me, motioning
to the dark
men.
"We have work to do you and I. Come, look sharp Watson. We don't have much time!"
He sets off
down the London
street, keeping to
the shadows. I
am following him
before it hits
me that I
must have entered
the book. I
wonder what the
night will bring.

The Hedgehog and its Wisdom

He sat down
beside me. I
just wanted to
enjoy the sun
and the read
book. Besides, I
didn't like him.
When he found
out I was
gay, he grimaced
and said in
a gruff voice

   We are all allowed to make our own choices in life.

I stared back
at him in
disbelief. I ignored
him, hoping that
he would go
away. But he
was trying to
get my attention.

   Look! He must like you, he's coming so close!

What are you talking about?

I asked trying
to keep the
bitterness out of
my words, but
not succeeding very
well at all.

There, right there. He's not afraid of you.

I looked to
where he was
pointing and saw
a chubby groundhog.
It was looking
at me with
eyes that seemed
to be filled
with soft wisdom.
We regard each
other for a
moment, the hedgehog
and I. Then
it ambles off
along the grass
looking for food.
The man next
to me smiles.

You must be a good person if animals like you. I've never seen a wild animal so unafraid. You must have magic in you.
I did not
know what to
say, so I
said absolutely nothing.

Kindle for My Fire

                                          What's that you've got there?

He pointed at
the eReader in
my lap but
his words were

                    deep

as if he
had some sort
bottomless well inside
of his stomach.

            It's a eReader

I said, wondering
where he had
come from. He
hadn't been there
before. I hadn't
heard him approach.

                                        What's that? What do you do with it?

                I read on it.

                                        Like a book? You don't get the tv or the phone on that? What do they call it?

> *A Kindle. It's just for reading, it doesn't do anything else.*

I wondered how,
in this day
and age, a
person couldn't know
of eReaders. What
must it be
like to live
without technology? Is
it a world
I could live
In? I wondered
and told him:

> *You read books on it. It's prefect for carrying around a lot of books. You can make the font bigger so you don't have to squint and hurt your eyes. You can even buy them with your eReader, if you want something new to read. I have twenty books on here.*

My enthusiasm
was not reciprocated.
I knew that
I had lost
him when he
gave me a
blank stare that
conveyed only confusion.
His eyes were
                         deep
with it, almost
                        bottomless
He mouth hung

in silent wonder
before he spoke
again. His voice
was as deep
as his eyes.

But a kindle is what you use for lighting a fire. Why would they call a book after something you burn? Didn't they think of that, when they made this thing? I want to read a book, I can just pick one up off the shelf.

He shuffled off
of the courtyard.
I wondered where
he had come
from and now
I watched him
go, my holding
my eReader closer
to my chest.

Mirror Twin

The day was
truncated, cut
in two. I
didn't know what
I was going
to do, how
I would fill
the hours now
that I was
suddenly alone. I
knew I would
get my chores
done, that I
would have them
done a day
early. But would
I be able
to sit down
at the computer
and write? It
was like being
constipated; the
words were there
but they wouldn't

come out. I
had managed to
write a shot
story, a few
poems. I told
myself that was
okay, at least
I was writing
something. Then I
thought back to
last year, with
over twenty releases,
writing and editing
all the time,
four or five
books on the
go at different
stages, even doing
graphic design. I
was once called
the "Wolf that
never sleeps" I
did so much.
Now, I can't
even summon up

the energy. I
can only write,
it's all I
have left. I
force myself to
sit at my
computer, like a
mirror version of
who I was,
what I used
to be capable
of. Like some
kind of mirror
twin, one from
past and one
in the present.
I sit and
I'm able to
squeeze out a
few words, the
linguistic equivalent of
hard rabbit turds.
Daily, I force
myself to write
my novel, even

if I don't
feel like writing.
I see it
as a hard
brick wall that
I have to
push my words
through, one at
a time. I
sit in front
of my computer,
its blinking eye
of a screen
staring at me,
waiting for the
feel of my fingers
on the keys.
Tonight, I manage
a whole scene.
I read back
over what I've
written, the voices
of my characters
speaking their words
loudly in my head:

"Please let me in! Please! Diane! Are you there?"

"Lady, what the fuck is going on here? Who the hell are you?"

"Oh god, now there are men dressed as woman out here! You have to help me! Let me in!"

"Oh no you didn't. Honey, who is this bitch anyway? Did she just say what I think she said? Bitch, do you know who I am?"

"A man in a dress."

"Bitch, I am not a man, I'm a hundred percent woman, here me roar!"

"Moira, get in here. You guys as well."

"Honey, that is some fucked up shit. Do you mind if I roll a joint? Don't worry, I promise I'll share."

For once, who

I was before

all of this

started to happen

is shining through.

The wall is

almost non-existent. I

can probably manage

a few pages.
The mirror twin
urges me on
as the words
flow out of
my fingers like
beautiful clear water,
and for a
moment, however long
it lasts, I
continue, letting the
words free, before
the wall becomes
opaque once more.

Courtyard Clattering

The courtyard was
made by five
buildings, all converging
in a small
square, about nine
by twelve, big
enough for a
few chairs and
a table. It
was surrounded by
a sea of
balconies like leaves
of a tree,
bird people and
noise. Some days,
I would get
a few spare
moments of quiet,
but this was
rare. I would
go outside with
a book and
wait. Usually only

a few minutes.

I was lucky

if I got two hours.

This evening, it

started right away.

> *What do you mean, you're going to be late?*
> *We have tickets to go out at seven.*
> *You can't be late.*
> **Silence**.
> *But we paid a lot of money for those tickets.*

So I told him that if he wanted me to do that, he had to propose to me first.
And what did he say? Oh my god, I can't believe you told him that.
Well, don't worry. He said he'd have to think about it. Can you believe him?
God, honey, men are such asshats!

My mother used to tell me, when I was a kid.
The reason why I have a dimple in my chin
is because God said "*And you learn to behave*
yourself, now stop it" **and poked me in the chin.**

Nah, the perfect movie to watch at Christmas time is Scrooged.
No, I want the classics, give me the Grinch and Rudolph any day.
What about Black Christmas? That's a good one.
That's not a good one. Are you fucking mental? I want sentimality at Christmas, not bloddy murder
I think you're ignoring the perfection of Scrooged. It's the perfect remake and becomes it's own movie and is STILL as heart warming as the original.
You both suck. Christmas is about tradition, it's about what you did as a kid that was magicl. Oh, A Christmas Story was also

*good. And a Charlie Brown Christmas. The first one though, not
the second one where the kids sounded all funny.*

You know that woman that used to live here?
Silence.
No, the one that looked like a man.
Silence.
No, the other one. The one that wore all those flowy dresses.
Silence.
No, that's not who I mean either. You know, the woman who lived
upstairs?
Silence.
Oh forget it, you have no idea who I'm talking about.

**So then my mother told me that
one of these days,** *"You're going
to hurt someone that really
matters to you."* **Well and now look
at what's happend. She left me.
She's left me and my mums
a phsycic. That's fucked up, man.**

The voices are

like a clattering

of birds inside

my head.

They are all

making a noise

that sounds like

its own kind

of music, but

I can't decide

If it's something
I can dance
dance to without
a real beat.

"I can't be your Harry Potter."

He said to
me. He pointed
at the tattoo
on my wrist.
"What do you mean?"
"That's where you go. He's who you want to be, to find in someone."
In actual fact,
it was Hermione
who was my
favourite character, I

heart

her. Harry's
story is the
stuff of legend
but if I
had to pick
a favourite character,
it would be
her. I turned
away from him.
"You wear his scar on your wrist."
He said. He

pointed at the
my tattoo again,
for a second
time. It looked
fresh in the
morning sun. There
were cars parking
and people talking.
A boys and
girls basketball team
had gotten off
a van, they let
out a cheer.
I wondered if
they had won
their tournament. Or
if they were
just about to
play. I couldn't
make it all
out, but it
was like a
war cry. It
sounded like
something said to

drum up courage.
It was a
sound that had
no spelling, that
had no discernible
words to me,
though I knew
that the sound
was composed of
words, that they
were hidden inside
of the sound.
"Because he wasn't defined by his scar. He rose above it, and became something great. Who doesn't dream of that?"
I thought for
a moment, tried
to think of
how to explain
it. Finally I
just told him.
"I don't want to date Harry Potter. That's not who I want in a man. Yes, I read Harry a lot, because I love the books."
I took a
breath, letting silence
work like punctuation.

"Harry Potter is one of my joys. I don't want to sleep with him. And, you know, that would be kind of gross, don't you think? I've known Harry since he was a kid."

I took another

breath, held it.

let it our.

I was silent.

"I can't be your Harry Potter."

He said again.

__Salutations__

>*See, this is why I didn't tell people, they give me that face*

She had just

told me she

was leaving, gone

before I knew

it, a spot

of brightness taken

from the day.

I didn't know. I said, *I would have gotten you a card.*
    That's nice. But I'll see you again. So I'll just say salutations.
Salutations?
  Yeah. Isn't that what the spider says to the pig in Charlottes web?
        You're the writer. Aren't you supposed to know this stuff?

She grinned and

I knew that

I would miss

her while she

was gone. Despite

only knowing her

in my life

during the day,

I thought of

her as a

true friend or

an every day

angel, those people

who come into

our lives for

a moment, or

two, sometimes years,

and they enrich

our lives, for

however short of

a time. They

leave it brighter.

Salutations, I said.

Chalice

It can take only seconds

to break the chalice.

That internal barrier that we

keep within. It is holds our

dreams, hopes, and wishes

and is very fragile.

Every time I fall,

my chalice breaks.

It shatters inside of me,

though my body just bruises.

I jingle with the clink

of broken glass.

Later, I'm able to shake

the glass from my skin. Soon I am

surrounded by pieces of glass,

shards of them, in a pretty

smoky blue hue. When I'm done,

I get my bottle of glue.

Every time I fall,

I glue the pieces of the

chalice back together.

<u>Endless Possibilities</u>

It's been a long time

since I've wanted to

get to know someone romantically.

Normally I'm confident,

unafraid, calm, centered.

That was before.

Now I carry something with me

internally and externally.

On the outside, there is

my third leg, the metal appendage

that helps me to get around.

On the inside, it is the unseen

that I carry with me, that shapes

how I walk, how I function.

The seen and unseen

shapes the first impression

the romantic interest has of me.

More often than not, they will

take one look at third leg made of metal

and want nothing to do with me.

When they find out what is unseen

inside of me, most want less than nothing

to do with me. But every once upon a time,

there will be one person who will see

beyond the seen and unseen, and only

see what is inside of my heart instead.

And then, the possibilities are endless.

A Winter Walk

I was walking in the snow.

my every movement

was focused only on

putting one foot

in front of the other.

My cane was making

star patterns in the

white crust on the earth.

A man approached me,

his face full of concern.

He said something

that I did not hear.

I asked him to repeat

himself. It didn't help

that the wind was blowing

and I had gone temporarily deaf.

He spoke again and I just nodded,

still not able to make out his words.

I walked on, thinking on him

and what he said came into me

loud and clear:

"Watch where you're going.

It's dangerous out! You have

to be careful."

I wish I had responded

with a thank you or

a smile, but I didn't hear him.

I heard him now

and his words kept me safe

on the long walk home.

The Mirror Though the Trees

When I glance in the mirror,

I see him.

He is a darker version of me,

one that is still unbeautiful

even though he's made

from silver glass and light.

He is the twin that I used to know,

never far from me,

hiding inside of me.

He starts speaking to me

in a soft, salient hiss

filled with loathing and

a subtle kind of sadness.

I imagine his hiss is the

soft rustle of leaves,

sprouting from trees that

I have conjured behind the glass.

Soon, the mirror looks out at

a sea of green, trees as far

as the eye can see,

each branch holding a wish

of possibilities undiscovered.

A lone bird, yellow feathers

that are streaked with white,

flies out of the mirror towards me,

his song bright like the sunshine.

He flies merrily around me,

his merry tune mixing

with the rustle of the leaves.

When I turn back to the mirror,

I see the dark twin is gone.

So is my bedroom.

All there is to be seen

is a sea of green leaves,

bending this way and that

in a breeze that almost seems

to be talking to me.

The Winds of Change

The winds of change

are a constant presence.

We do not know where

they will take us

or what they will bring.

The only thing we can do

is to embrace the wind

and learn from what

it shows us, what it teaches.

Though it seems like

we are leaving something behind,

we are actually taking

everything we learned with us.

So that when the next wind arrives,

when the winds embrace us again,

we will be ready.

Chanel No. 5 and the Sound of Winter

I walked to the bus stop.

The cold and biting wind

sliced

into me. It

bit

into me, it's teeth like

needles

in my skin.

When I arrived at the bus stop,

I was alone. Then I turned and

a Lady was there. She was

dressed in a thick over coat

made of a dark wool that matched

the colour of her fur hat.

The Lady had dark black hair

that came down on her left side,

framing her face like wings.

"It's so terribly cold." She said. "Are you wearing a warm winter coat?"
I looked at her and smiled.

She seemed harmless enough.

"The coat I'm wearing is wool. My parents got it for me."

The Lady took in my appearance,

nodded as if satisfied.

"You're parents are very wonderful. But you need a better hat."
She smiled, as if she were filled

with a heat despite the cold.

"Do you want to smell something that will warm you up?"
Oddly enough, She pulled out

a crumpled tissue.

She held it up to my nose.

"It's Chanel No. 5."

She shrugged her shoulders.

"There are people who say that it's an old scent, that it makes you smell like an old fart, but then they're the one's who've forgotten about Marilyn."
She held out the tissue again

"Smell it. It will take you back. There is a real class to it. I do hope there aren't any additives. But it smells so lovely. It makes you remember, you know? I still remember the first time I smelled Chanel No. 5."

I didn't,

but the scent of it,

beautiful and distinctive,

gave me a brief blast of warmth.

It was soft and soothing,

like a blanket.

She took the tissue back

and smiled at me again.

I noticed a small tear form

at the edge of her eye.

With all of the make up that

she was wearing, it sat there

like a jewel perched on upon

black velvet. Her eyes were painted

a green so that they looked like leaves.

"Do you want a clean tissue?"

I asked her. There had to be

something that I could say

or should say to her.

She shook her head and

the tear slid down her face,

leaving a mark running though

her softly blushed cheeks.

"No, dear. It's okay. I just want to make sure you get home safely. I think it's coming there now, look, see? It's a little further back?"
She pointed with a black

gloved hand into the distance.

"*See?*" She said.

I nodded and we waited for

the bus to stop in front of us.

When it did, I got on and turned

to the well dressed Lady.

She wasn't there.

All that was there

was the scent of

Chanel No. 5

and the sound of winter.

The Brightest of Souls

I got onto the bus and

all the seats were full.

I resigned myself to standing

but when a woman saw me,

she stood up quickly

and tried to gave me her seat.

The woman had a stroller

in front of her, the baby

was within it, cooing away.

"No," I said. "That's okay.

I can stand fine, you sit

with your baby."

A man got up from

his seat. "You sit down."

He said to the woman.

"You sit here." He pointed

at me then at his seat.

When I sat down,

the child's eyes followed me.

There was an older woman

sitting next to me and she

tapped me on the arm.

"That child notices you."

She said. "Children always

notice the brightest of souls."

She gestured at the child.

"This child is very taken with you."

I looked at him. He was very small

in a very big stroller. He was wearing

a red and white winter coat.

Blond curls poked out from

beneath a thick hat.

I waved at him. "Hello." I said.

"Hello there. Aren't you a cutie."

I was rewarded with an instant smile

that filled the front of the bus

with brightness more brilliant

than sunshine. When he laughed,

it grew brighter. I waved at him

and talked to him some more,

each laugh he gave me

was like the tinkle of bells.

As I got off the bus, I turned

to watch it drive away.

The bus looked as if

it were filled with brilliant

and beautiful sun. It now

filled the whole bus until

everything was visible.

I saw the child waving as the

bus drove away,

a trail of the suns rays

behind it like a tail.

The Broken Man

He gave me a gift.

I was expecting a ring,

something to symbolize

the bond that was between us.

What I got instead was

a pack of tarot cards.

They had names I had

never seen before.

Instead of normal cards

like the Lovers or the Heirophant,

the Fool or the Tower,

there were cards like

the Lost Soul, the Forgotten One

and The Broken Man.

"That's you." He said.

He pointed to The Broken Man.

"That's you as you are now."

The card depicted a man

made of glass. His feet

and legs were shatters of glass,

littering the ground like

diamonds turned to dust.

His face was a mask of pain,

whether internal or external

I did not know.

I didn't feel broken inside,

though I was approaching

that eventuality.

I didn't want to be

The Broken Man. I felt like

The Gingerbread Man, my

breakable legs one step away

from being cookie crumbs.

I took the cards up to a cliff.

It overlooked the whole world

and I could see the land

stretching in front of me.

I could feel the world behind me.

I stood on a precipice,

my life before and

my life after. I only had to choose.

I raised my hand holding the cards

to the wind and let it take

the cards from my hand.

As they swirled away,

flying out of my hand,

I saw The Broken Man.

Instead of pain on his face,

he was smiling.

As the cards flew from my grasp,

I knew I had made

the right decision.

I was the Broken Man

no longer

Sword and Sanctuary

I held the letter in my hand.

It was waiting for me

when I arrived home.

I knew that he had left it for me,

one last gift or something

made to hurt. Perhaps

a little bit of both-

he was good at that.

His gifts came with strings,

his counsel came a price,

and his company with

sacrifice.

In the letter,

he told me that he had

moved on, he had found

someone better than me.

It was like a knife.

with only one purpose.

I'd finally let him go.

He was like holding on to

brambles and thorns,

that took blood from me

as payment.

To get away from him,

I had fought against the

thorns he offered and hid

inside the forest,

in the branches of the trees

looking out until he

had gone away.

It was fitting that

his last words to me

cut like a sword.

That he sliced into me

as I had done to him.

I'd cut him out

to save myself.

I stood, holding the letter,

running a finger along

it's sharp edges.

The cut was fast, like a blade.

The paper became bloody

in seconds,

the shape of trees formed

on the paper drawn in my ink.

The trees were shaped

like the forest I had hid inside.

The branches were moving

on the paper.

Intense heat ran through me.

It wasn't anger, just the knowledge

that the forest was no longer safe.

It was done providing sanctuary.

My hand grew warm.

When the flame erupted,

in the middle of my palm,

I was not afraid.

The burning of the paper

like the crackling of leaves,

brief and quick.

The letter was simply

ashes now.

When I blew the ashes away,

the cut on my finger was gone.

I took the sword that he

had offered to me

and used it to

cut him

away.

These Words and I

I don't understand the question.

Words are garbled to me,

going in and coming out.

Twice yesterday, I went to speak,

and words that I hadn't meant to say

came out instead.

When I'm speaking, it as if

my words aren't my own.

Sometimes, I go to speak and words

that are best left behind a filter

of some sort come out unbidden,

as if they were lying in wait.

As I say them, I try to push them back in,

try to stop the flow coming

from my mouth, try to quickly

build the barrier up again.

It is the inside voice

that we usually keep hidden.

I struggle to make sense of them,

these shapes that make letters,

those letters forming words.

I used to know them so well,

we used to be on good terms.

We got along famously,

wrote together, spoke together,

told stories together,

these words and I.

Now I wonder if I will

ever know them

that well again.

Decowled

During the night

I dream of myself.

I am wearing a cowl

that covers my face.

I am in a room

made entirely of stone.

There are candles that

flicker with light and shadow.

A woman approaches me

with her hands held out.

"I knew you would come to see me"
She says. Her eyes are a deep violet,

her smile warm. She radiates light.

"How did you know I would be here?"
I ask her. Though I have never been here

and do not know the woman,

I don't feel any fear. Only a sense of calm.

"I always know when those seeking answers will arrive."
She shrugs.

"It is the way."
She sits and I do the same,

sitting across from her.

She takes my hands in hers

and I experience only a warmth

that drives away the chill

of the stone room.

"You wish to know if you are on the right path?"

"Yes."
I whisper.

"How did you know?"

"You have an inquisitive spirit. It is written on your face."

I say nothing, the truth of her words

ringing inside of me, as if my body

is agreeing to her words with

every fibre of its being.

"You are on the right path, but you must look where you are going."
She squeezes my hands.

"To do that, you must see."
She reaches up and pulls the cowl

down off my head.

The room we are in is transformed

from cold hard stone to a field of grass.

Trees and blue sky surround us.

I wonder if it was there all along.

"Do not be afraid of seeing, of taking hold of what you want."
She begins to fade, her violet eyes

becoming a misty gray.

"You must remain true to yourself."
Bright sun fills the grass covered room,

more brilliant than the sun.

My eyes open in the darkness

but a shadow of the bright light remains,

infusing everything I see.

=

The Querent

For Trevour Strudwick for the title of this poem and the teachings behind it.

The cards wanted to sing to me.

I wanted to open the portal

to the possible,

and what I had to know.

Each card was a window,

into another world.

They showed the possible.

The were keys to

the mystery that was life.

They filled my world with

Fire, Water, Air and Earth

Wands, Cups, Swords and Disks.

I went to them,

and took them from

within silk and wood.

I held them and asked

what I needed to know.

Then I lay them down,

and read what they

had to say to me.

The Empress

Dedicated to Dawn who is an Empress.

The things she held on to

were like photographs

that danced around her

like dreams which

everyone could see.

She held love in one hand

and mercy in the other.

She held tight to sexuality

and emotion,

letting the two

mingle and meld and mix.

She held on to the smoke they created

like a wish waiting

to be born.

She was the beginning

of all life,

the power of nature

and what it could

give back to the world.

She was change and renewal

and the embodiment of passion,

filling the air around her

with joy and reflection.

She was Mother Nature,

creating a new connection

between the visible

and the invisible.

Looking around her,

She saw that each of

these parts of her

were represented by pictures

and only by stepping back

could you look

at the whole of her.

She was the Empress

with her head turned

towards the future.

A Side of Chalice with Dinner

I met him out front,

not willing yet to take him

into my sanctum sanctorum.

He hadn't earned that right yet.

I didn't know him,

that was the point of meeting.

I knew things would not

work out in my favour

when he looked at me.

His eyes were cold and

there was no light within.

He gave me an up and down look,

taking me all in

and dismissing me right away.

"You don't look like your pictures." He said.

"How can I not?" I said. **"They're pictures of me."**
"Well for one thing, you didn't have that."
He made a hand flipping motion

as if he wanted to shoo the cane away.

"You didn't tell me you walked with one of those."
"Should that make a difference?"
"Yes. I don't want to date half a man. What's going on with that?"
"I told you. I have MS."
"You said you were on meds. I assumed that meant you were cured."
I was stunned, shocked, and felt the

chalice breaking into pieces.

It was different this time though.

It wasn't shattering.

It was preparing for battle.

We walked to the restaurant,

the wind and cold slicing into me,

as if the wind carried knifes.

The chalice inside of me

was also breaking into shards,

long pieces that I could feel in my mouth,

pressing against my tongue and cheeks.

We sat down to dinner and ordered.

I didn't know why I was here.

He had seemed so nice when

we had spoken before, so kind.

His true self was shining through however.

"So, how long have you had MS?"
"Since January of last year."
"Must be kind of shitty. Living a half life."
"I live a full life. I love my life."
"How can you love your life if you have MS?"
His voice was cold and dismissive.

"That's not a life, that's a death sentence."
"You have no idea what you're talking about."
The shards of the chalice had found their way out.

They lodged themselves into his face.

Though he didn't know they were there,

I could see them shining brightly,

catching the light like after thoughts.

**"It's made me more grateful for the small things.
It's made me a better person because everything I do is a victory.
It's helped me learn a lot about me and I love myself."**
"Good thing you do, no one will love you with that monkey on your back."
I sat there stunned at his words.

I had struggled all year to find peace.

I would not let one man determine my self love.

**"You're wrong. There's lots of love in my life.
I love myself, I have family and friends who love me,**

who know me. And I love myself. That's what matters."
He scoffed. *"You love yourself. How quaint."*
I motioned to the waiter.

"Can you wrap my food to go please?"
"You're not leaving are you. We haven't even had dinner."
"I'm going to have dinner. At home."
"We're on a date!"
He was outraged that I was daring to leave.

**"I'm stronger than you. I'm a better person than you.
I'm a different person and I love who I've become.
I don't need any of your bad vibes messing up
what I've worked to hard to gain."**
"And what is that? What can a half man like you have gained?"
I thought about it for a moment

but the answer was there waiting to be spoken.

"I found myself." I said.
I took my food from the waiter

and turned to look at him.

He looked as if he was covered

in shards of ice.

I flicked my hand and the shards

of the chalice came back to me,

slipping into place so that the chalice

was whole once more.

"Have a nice life. I know I will."

I walked home, feeling the joy

of my own making filling my body,

keeping me warm against the cold.

To Your Health

Everyone I knew or had known

was in a large banquet hall.

I was surrounded by those

I loved, even people that I

had not seen in years.

and the hall was filled with

the sound of people talking.

Their voices were like music.

I had no idea why we were there;

it was like I had woken up

all of a sudden only to find myself

surrounded by a Shangri-La of

friends and family.

I was sitting in a throne that

was in the centre of the room.

The party was going on around me,

and I was as it's centre. It was as if

I was the sun and the people

I loved were the planets.

A woman stood up and

clinked the edge of her cup

with a long, pointed knife.

It looked like a sword.

The room fell silent and

everyone was expectant.

"We all know why we're here."

She smiled at me and raised

her glass. She was shining and bright,

like the moon, full of light that

rippled all over her skin

and made her sparkle.

"We're here to celebrate you."

She pointed at me and I was filled

with love and contentment.

"We have a gift for you."

She held up large piece of paper.

On it, I saw myself as I was

when I was younger.

It was a photograph

that had been blown up to full size.

I looked at my younger self

and recognized myself there,

even though I no longer felt

like the same person.

She pulled out something

that looked like a wand.

Waving it in front of the paper,

I watched the photo begin to

shimmer and undulate.

I watched the photograph

settle itself on the paper

as if it were a Polaroid.

When the picture started

to came into focus,

I saw myself as I was now,

holding out two gold disks,

one balanced in each palm.

"Who you were has changed

into who you are."

She pointed with her wand at

the paper again and it began

to shimmer once more,

When it came into focus,

I saw myself again.

I was standing on a grassy knoll,

looking towards the future,

surrounded by the sun and sky.

The disks from the previous photo

had multiplied and surrounded me.

They were floating in the sky

like several small suns.

There were animals in the grass.

They looked as if they were protecting me,

or offering me guidance on the journey

that I was about to take into the unknown.

"You are not afraid of yourself anymore."

She smiled again and her brightness

increased until it looked

as if she were made of stars.

She raised her glass and said "To your health!"

Everyone in the room raised their own glass

and repeated the words.

They clinked their glasses

their neighbours and the room

sounded as if it were filled

with the tinkling of bells.

Light began to pour from their cups

until all I could see was

was the brightness

of the sun.

Another Turn on the Wheel

Dedicated to Jackie O'Grady, who is a bright shining sun.

Another year

wiser, stronger, confident.

Another spoke on the wheel

that turns and marks

our passage through time.

There is a light that shines

from inside of you,

brightening the life

of anyone that comes

into your sphere.

The world is more glorious

with you in it.

You are Goddess personified,

grace made real,

beauty given form.

You are a beacon of

wonderful glorious light

that shines freely,

brightening even

the darkest of days.

Bjork Over Beer

Dedicated to the always fabulous Erin Dowe, who loves Bjork as much as I do.

She sat across from me,

the sparkles under her eyes

catching the light like

little stars that brightened

and faded as the light

shone on them

"When I saw you this summer at the Bjork concert, you were so different than how you used to be. You were soft spoken and mild mannered."

I remembered.

I took a sip of beer,

it's darkness in contrast

to the brightness I

held inside of me.

"I was a different person then. I was bogged down with everything, with how to handle it, with what my life had become."

She looked at me

over the rim of her glass,

"What changed for you? I mean, now you're who you were, you're swearing, you have life in you again, you've got it going on and you're back to your fabulous self."

I thought about it

for a moment,

unsure how to articulate

what I wanted to say.

"I had two choices. I could wallow and give up, or I could live. I chose to live. I'm a different person now, but so much better for it."

She clinked my glass,

the sound like bells

and I wondered if an angel

would get it's wings.

"I'll drink to that. It's good to have you back."

I smiled and drank,

the beer cool in my throat.

"It's good to be back. I'm not going to go away again."

I took another sip of beer

and thought about how

my life had changed.

I realised then that

the lightness inside of me

had a name. It was

happiness

and I promised myself

that I would always carry

it with me.

Petals on the Wind

Dedicated to the wonderful Heather Garrod, who helped with the flowers.

I clicked on the computer. It

powered on but it wasn't my

home screen that appeared.

Instead it was a sea of flowers:

          apple blossoms,

          daisies,

          dandelions,

          chrysanthemums,

          lavender

          and orchids.

They glowed for

a moment, brightening

the screen. There was a

buzz of electricity,

a blue spark.

As I watched

the flowers began

to slide out

from under the glass.

A breeze came with them

and blew the flower petals

around my room. They

swirled around me,

and I stood in a

whirlwind of colour.

The petals slipped

out of an open window

and I ran after them,

leaving my apartment

and going out

into the light.

The petals were

were waiting for me.

As I approached them,

they began to

flow around me,

pulsing with light

and warmth. They

began to dance

away from me,

and flew to the sky,

forming a long, straight line,

with a point at the end,

a long plume of colour

on a canvass of

clear blue sky.

A few of them remained,

floating around me

like a wish in the air

after it has been spoken.

I followed the arrow

in the sky

to a meadow that

I had never seen before.

It was covered in flowers

of the same

jewel like hues.

Standing in the

middle of the

meadow was

you.

When I went

closer to

you,

and took your hand

in mine, the flower petals

moved and surged around

us, pulsing with

light, matched only

by the brightness

that shone from

inside of

you.

About the Author

Jamieson is an award winning, Number One Best Selling Author of over sixty books.

He is also an accomplished artist. He works in mixed media, charcoal, pastels and oil paints. Jamieson is also something of an amateur photographer and graphic designer.

He currently lives in Ottawa Ontario Canada with his cat, Tula, who is fearless.

Learn more about Jamieson at www.JamiesonWolf.com

www.ingramcontent.com/pod-product-compliance
Lightning Source LLC
LaVergne TN
LVHW022322080426
835508LV00041B/1795